LET'S FIND OUT! TRANSPORTATION

ALL ABOUT TRAINS

JUSTINE CIOVACCO

Britannica Educational Publishing
IN ASSOCIATION WITH
ROSEN
EDUCATIONAL SERVICES

Published in 2017 by Britannica Educational Publishing (a trademark of Encyclopædia Britannica, Inc.) in association with The Rosen Publishing Group, Inc.
29 East 21st Street, New York, NY 10010

Distributed exclusively by Rosen Publishing.
To see additional Britannica Educational Publishing titles, go to rosenpublishing.com.

First Edition

Britannica Educational Publishing
J.E. Luebering: Executive Director, Core Editorial
Mary Rose McCudden: Editor, Britannica Student Encyclopedia

Rosen Publishing
Christine Poolos: Editor
Nelson Sá: Art Director
Nicole Russo: Designer
Cindy Reiman: Photography Manager
Sherri Jackson: Photo Researcher

Library of Congress Cataloging-in-Publication Data

Names: Ciovacco, Justine, author.
Title: All about trains / Justine Ciovacco.
Description: First edition. | New York : Britannica Educational Publishing in association with Rosen Educational Services, 2017. | Series: Let's find out! Transportation | Includes bibliographical references and index.
Identifiers: LCCN 2015048711| ISBN 9781680484465 (library bound : alk. paper) | ISBN 9781680484540 (pbk. : alk. paper) | ISBN 9781680484236 (6-pack : alk. paper)
Subjects: LCSH: Railroad trains--Juvenile literature. | Railroads--Juvenile literature. | Railroad travel--Juvenile literature.
Classification: LCC TF148 .C4935 2017 | DDC 625.2--dc23
LC record available at http://lccn.loc.gov/2015048711

Photo credits: Cover, p. 1 Pagina/Shutterstock.com; p. 4 Hans-Peter Merten/robertharding/Getty Images; p. 5 Pavel L Photo and Video/Shutterstock.com; p. 6 Albert Pego/Shutterstock.com; p. 7 narvikk/E+/Getty Images; p. 8 Sergey Bogdanov/Shutterstock.com; p. 9 Gerald Bernard/Shutterstock.com; p. 10 De Agostini Picture Library/Getty Images; p. 11 Danita Delimont/Gallo Images/Getty Images; p. 12 Omikron/Science Source/Getty Images; p. 13 Leonid Andronov/Shutterstock.com; p. 14 Vdovichenko Denis/Shutterstock.com; p. 15 Charles Briscoe-Knight/Photographer's Choice/Getty Images; p. 16 Luis Davilla/Photolibrary/Getty Images; p. 17 Stan Honda/AFP/Getty Images; p. 18 Alexander Spatari/Moment/Getty Images; p. 19 Robin MacDougall/Photographer's Choice/Getty Images; p. 20 Liu Jin/AFP/Getty Images; p. 21 Othk/Asia Images/Getty Images; p. 22 Stephen Collector/Photographer's Choice/Getty Images; p. 23 Jeff Wilson/Shutterstock.com; p. 24 Takeshi Ishikawa/EyeEm/Getty Images; p. 25 Ulrich Baumgarten/Getty Images; p. 26 Keith Levit/Shutterstock.com; p. 27 EdStock/Getty Images; p. 28 Karl Johaentges/Look-foto/Getty Images; p. 29 Ulrik Tofte/DigitalVision/Thinkstock; interior pages background image ChaiyonS021/Shutterstock.com

Contents

Coming Down the Tracks

Trains carry passengers and freight all over the world.

One of the fastest ways for many people to travel together over land is by train. Trains travel along a path of two metal rails, or tracks. Each section of the train is linked together. The wheels on the bottom have a slightly curved outer edge. That is what makes them stay on the rails.

There are two types of trains: passenger and freight. Passenger trains carry people. Freight trains carry products.

Railroads have been essential to the spread of people settling across many countries, including the United States. Today, trains help people travel across almost every country in the world. Railroads serve many thousands of communities, from big cities to tiny villages in faraway areas.

THINK ABOUT IT

A bus is another way many people can travel together on land. Why would one travel by train rather than bus?

Passenger trains allow people to sit back and enjoy the sights while traveling.

Trains on the Run

Railroads were designed to move large amounts of passengers or things over long distances. They are the most efficient method of land transportation because they require the least amount of fuel and work by people.

A locomotive is the vehicle that pulls most trains. It can be powered by an engine that burns diesel fuel or by

Something that works well and does not waste time or resources is **efficient**.

A driver in a diesel locomotive operates the train with help from a crew of people.

The inside of a locomotive has computers and controls. The engineer must be trained to ensure a safe ride for all.

electricity. The electricity comes from a third rail or an overhead wire.

The train operator, called the driver or engineer, usually sits in the locomotive. Some modern trains have computers that help guide the train and control its speed. The engineer uses the computers and other devices to run the train. Those devices include a throttle, reversing gear, and brake. The throttle controls the locomotive's speed. The reversing gear allows the train to back up. The brake controls slowing and stopping.

The wheels of a train allow the cars to move smoothly along the rails.

Think About It

Most trains have drivers. Why is it important to have people as well as computers operating them?

Each section of a train is called a car. The underside of a railroad car is called an undercarriage. It holds the wheels. Under each end of a car are couplers. They look like hooks. Their job is to connect the cars.

A train runs on rails, or tracks. They guide the train and help spread the weight of the train on the ground. Tracks usually have two parallel steel rails. They are spaced 4 feet 8.5 inches (1.44 meters) apart. The rails are connected by wood or concrete pieces called crossties.

Railroad tracks can split off into different paths so they can cover more ground to get people and things where they need to go.

The rails are bolted down to the crossties. The ties sit on loose gravel or another material that provides a cushioned, steady foundation.

The rails have switches at some points. Switches are devices that can move the tracks to shift the path of the train.

Tracking Train History

Horse-drawn trains traveled the tracks of the Baltimore and Ohio railway in 1829.

People used horses to pull carts along tracks before there were modern trains. Europeans began using this early type of animal-led railroad in the 1500s. It allowed them to carry heavy loads to and from mines, where workers dug up coal and other minerals.

In 1803 British engineer Richard Trevithick planned and

George Stephenson's Rocket steam locomotive is pictured with a driver at the controls in 1829.

built a locomotive that ran on steam power. Mining companies were the first to use it. In the 1820s another British inventor, George Stephenson, made the first steam train to carry products and passengers. It was called the Rocket. Soon railroads were being built all over Europe. George Stephenson and his son Robert continued to try to improve the steam locomotive so it would run faster and smoother.

Compare and Contrast

Horses pulled cars on tracks before steam engines were invented. What problems might horses have that trains with engines do not have?

Union Pacific Railroad workers team up to lay tracks near Laramie, Wyoming, in 1868.

In the United States, the first railroads connected cities in the eastern part of the country. In 1862 the government gave money to two companies to build a route across the country. The Central Pacific laid track eastward from Sacramento, California. The Union Pacific built westward from Omaha, Nebraska. They met in Promontory, Utah, in May 1869. This was the first transcontinental railroad.

Electric locomotives were introduced in 1895. They receive power through overhead wires or third rails connected to central power stations. In 1925 U.S.

Some locomotives are powered by electricity that comes from wires above the train.

railroads started to use an electric diesel locomotive that carried its own power source.

Diesel engines are still used all over the world. However, some of the busiest railroads—including those in the United States, Europe, Russia, and Japan—use electricity from a central source. Some less developed countries still use steam locomotives.

Think About It

Many Native Americans were forced to move from their homelands when the railroads were built on their land. Was it fair to make them move?

Building a Path

The first U.S. railroads started near East Coast cities with seaports, where goods traveled in and out of the country. Trains connected these cities, so more people could receive these goods. By the mid-1850s, railroad tracks had been extended to reach other cities to the west. Some tracks even connected parts of the United States to Canada.

Building railroads takes a lot of work. First someone has to decide what route the railroad should take. There are many other issues to address as well. Trees may have to be

Cargo shipped to ports is loaded onto trains for another journey.

Think About It

The United States has not had much new track construction in recent years. Why might that be?

cut down. Tunnels need to be cut through mountains. Bridges need to be built to span rivers. When the land is ready, the track is laid by hand or by machines. After railroad tracks are built, they need a lot of care and frequent repairs.

Trains can carry people and goods almost anywhere. They can even go through mountains!

HELPING PEOPLE ON THE MOVE

Passenger trains have cars with seats. Trains that cover long distances have dining cars, baggage cars, and even sleeping cars with beds. The speed of many large passenger trains is about 100 miles (160 kilometers) per hour. However, some trains in Europe and Japan can go much faster.

Other trains carry people shorter distances. These trains

A **passenger** is a person riding in a vehicle.

On some trains, people traveling long distances can enjoy a drink or meal in an elegant dining car.

Subways run underground to carry people around large crowded cities.

often do not have a separate locomotive. Instead, some or all of the cars have electric motors under the floor. The train operator sits in the front car. These include commuter trains (trains that carry workers into a city), subways (underground trains), and monorails (trains that run on one rail).

Commuter trains have cars that carry as many people as possible. Some commuter cars have two levels of seats and can carry as many as 150 passengers. Thousands of people can be on one train.

Riding the Bullet

In the 1900s some countries began building trains that could go much faster than ordinary trains. Japan's bullet train was the world's first high-speed train. It began operating on October 1, 1964. The name of the train is the Shinkansen. It was built to travel from Tokyo to Osaka but has since been extended. These trains can travel up to 177 miles (285 kilometers) per hour.

The Shinkansen glides into a station in Kyoto, Japan. This high-speed train is one of the world's fastest.

THINK ABOUT IT

Why do countries want to build trains that can run very fast?

France's high-speed trains are known as the TGV. One train set a new world speed record of 320 miles (515 kilometers) per hour in 1990, but the trains usually run slower than that. The TGV trains are powered by front and rear electric locomotives.

Many other countries have high-speed trains or are planning to build them. In the United States, the Acela is a high-speed train service that runs from Boston, Massachusetts, to Baltimore, Maryland. These trains travel up to 150 miles (241 kilometers) per hour. Super-fast train lines are planned for many other parts of the country, too.

France's TGV holds the current world record for the fastest single ride.

The Magic of Maglevs

Magnetic levitation, or maglev, trains are the world's fastest trains. Maglevs do not have wheels moving on rails. Instead, magnetic coils in the surface of the track create a system that lifts the vehicles and moves them forward. The ride is smoother than an ordinary train. Speeding up and slowing down are faster because the train's bottom never touches the track. Bad weather usually has no effect on this train's movement.

In 2004 China's Shanghai Transrapid became the world's first commercial

The world's first maglev train is used by many people in Shanghai, China.

Think About It

New technology makes trains more expensive to build. Why is new technology important?

maglev train line—and the world's fastest at the time. It operates in China's most populated city, Shanghai. It runs at a speed of 267 miles (430 kilometers) per hour.

Japan is now testing maglev trains, called Lo trains, that may travel more than 300 miles (480 kilometers) per hour. When the trains start running in 2027, a ride that now takes 90 minutes will take only 40 minutes.

The tracks of a maglev train look different from traditional railroad tracks.

Making Things Move

Many trains carry goods rather than people. These are called **freight** trains. Boxcars carry packaged goods or other freight that must be protected from the weather. Some are cushioned to protect fragile shipments from damage. Open-top hopper

A freight train carries heavy loads of coal in open cars across the landscape of the American West.

Freight means goods or cargo carried by ship, train, truck, or airplane.

cars can carry minerals, such as coal or iron ore. Covered hopper cars carry grain. Tank cars carry liquids. Car carriers carry automobiles. Flatcars are open with no side panels. They can carry large, heavy materials, such as lumber and construction equipment.

Freight trains can have 150 or more cars. These trains usually move more slowly than passenger trains because they pull so much weight.

A double-stack container train can carry double the amount of goods.

Companies that run freight trains compete with highway trucking companies to get other companies to pay them to move their products. Some freight trains now have cars stacked on top of each other and specialized cars to carry liquid chemicals or refrigerated items.

Keeping Track of Trains

The world has more than 738,000 miles (1,187,000 kilometers) of railroad tracks. Almost all railroads carry both freight and passengers. So how do all these trains travel without crashing?

At first, railroad companies used a timetable system. A timetable shows the time when each train is scheduled to arrive at each station and which trains have the right to move through first.

Traffic signals tell trains when to stop and go. They also warn cars when a train is approaching.

Today there are more modern ways to keep trains running safely. One way trains stay safe is with the use of signals, including lights. These signals are controlled by people in signaling centers. The signals themselves work a lot like the traffic lights that control cars on the road. They help train operators know traffic that is coming up. Operators also use radios and computers to study traffic.

Compare and Contrast

Early train networks used only used the timetable system. Why is it more helpful to use signals, too?

Workers in signaling centers monitor train traffic and send signals to operators.

Train Hall of Fame

The Orient-Express provided a comfortable and luxurious travel experience for passengers.

Trains and their trips may become famous thanks to their speed, their history, or just the scenes they show off. Here are a few interesting trains.

The Baltimore and Ohio was the first public railroad built in the United States. It began operating in 1830.

Between 1883 and 1977, the Orient Express regularly took passengers from Paris, France, to Istanbul, Turkey. The **luxury** train carried royalty and the very rich.

Since 1898, the Trans-Siberian Express has made the longest regular train trip in the world. It travels from Moscow to Vladivostok, Russia. That's 5,778 miles (9,299 kilometers) in nine days!

Luxury means comfortable, rich surroundings.

A train called the Mallard holds the record for the fastest steam locomotive. In 1938 it reached a speed of almost 126 miles (203 kilometers) per hour.

The Qinghai-Tibet Railway has the world's highest track. It connects Tibet with other parts of China. The train travels over a mountain pass that is 16,640 feet (5,072 meters) above sea level.

The high-climbing Qinghai-Tibet Railway stocks an oxygen supply for each passenger.

The End of the Line

Trains have been making life easier for people since the early 1800s. Today many people take airplanes rather than trains for long-distance trips. Trains continue to be popular ways to travel, however.

Each year billions of people ride trains to work. In 2013 more than a billion and a half people rode the subways and train lines in New York

City kids who ride subways to school might do their homework, take naps, and eat snacks on the trains.

A train ride gives families the chance to relax together while someone else does the driving.

City, Mexico City, Hong Kong, and Paris. That same year, more than 3 billion people rode the subway in Tokyo and in Beijing!

THINK ABOUT IT

Why do some people still prefer to take a train rather than a plane for a long trip?

Other people take trains for fun. In some places it is still possible to ride old steam trains. These are popular for several reasons. Some people just enjoy seeing and feeling what it is like to ride an old train. Others enjoy the sites they can see from the trains.

GLOSSARY

brake A device for slowing or stopping a moving vehicle such as a bicycle, car, or train.

commuters People who travel back and forth between home and work or school regularly.

freight Goods that are carried from one place to another by vehicle.

gear A device that adjusts the movement of a machine.

levitation The rising or lifting of a person or thing.

locomotive An engine that moves under its own power, especially one that moves cars on a railroad.

parallel Lying or moving in the same direction and staying always the same distance apart.

products Something produced or made.

rails Bars of steel forming a track for wheeled vehicles.

repair To fix or make able to work again.

reverse Go backwards.

route An established, selected, or assigned course of travel.

section A part of a whole.

signals Sounds or motions made to give warning or command.

subways Underground electric railways.

switch A device made usually of movable rails that allows a train or streetcar to move from one track to another.

technology The use of science in solving problems.

throttle A handle or valve controlling the flow of steam or fuel to an engine.

tracks The course along which something moves.

undercarriage A supporting structure or underside.

For More Information

Books

Clapper, Nikki. *Freight Trains* (All Aboard!). North Mankato, MN: Capstone Press, 2015.

MacArthur, Colin. *Inside a High-Speed Train* (Life in the Fast Lane).New York, NY: Cavendish Square Publishing, 2014.

Nardo, Don. *The Golden Spike: How a Photograph Celebrated the Transcontinental Railroad.* North Mankato, MN: Capstone Press, 2015.

Otfinoski, Steven. *Building the Transcontinental Railroad: An Interactive Engineering Adventure.* North Mankato, MN: Capstone Press, 2014.

Otfinoski, Steven. *High-Speed Trains: From Concept to Consumer.* New York, NY: Scholastic, 2015.

Peters, Elisa. *Let's Ride the Subway!* New York, NY: PowerKids Press, 2014.

Websites

Because of the changing nature of Internet links, Rosen Publishing has developed an online list of websites related to the subject of this book. This site is updated regularly. Please use this link to access this list:

http://www.rosenlinks.com/LFO/train

Index